How to Build
EGYPTIAN
BOAT MODELS

Patterns and Instructions
for Three Royal Vessels

JACK SINTICH

DOVER PUBLICATIONS, INC.
MINEOLA, NEW YORK

This book is dedicated to
Judee, Tom, Tim, John, Kim, Jacob, and Joshua

Copyright

Copyright © 2007 by Jack Sintich
All rights reserved.

Bibliographical Note

How to Build Egyptian Boat Models: Patterns and Instructions for Three Royal Vessels is a new work, first published by Dover Publications, Inc., in 2007.

Library of Congress Cataloging-in-Publication Data

Sintich, Jack.
    How to build Egyptian boat models : patterns and instructions for three royal vessels / Jack Sintich.
        p. cm.
    ISBN-13: 978-0-486-45566-2 (pbk.)
    ISBN-10: 0-486-45566-1 (pbk.)
        1. Sailboats—Egypt—Models—History. I. Title.

VM359.S56 2007
623.82'011—dc22

                                                                2007003426

Manufactured in the United States of America
Dover Publications, Inc., 31 East 2nd Street, Mineola, N.Y. 11501

INTRODUCTION

In this book you will find detailed instructions on how to build three different ancient Egyptian boat models. The vessels are modeled after the royal sailing boats of three pharaohs: King Khufu (ruled ca. 2551–2528 B.C.); Queen Hatshepsut (ruled ca. 1479–1458 B.C.); and King Ramses II (ruled ca. 1279–1213 B.C.) These boats represent fine examples of the art and technology that was available during each particular pharaoh's reign. The scale of each model is one inch equals seven feet. The models are three-dimensional replicas of royal sailing galley images taken from temple stone carvings and tomb paintings found in the Valley of the Kings, an ancient Egyptian burial site.

Even a beginner can construct these royal sailing boats. Model builders from ages nine to adult will find the instructions and patterns easy to understand, easy to copy, and most important—great fun to construct!

The hobbyist building these royal boat models will be following the process that the ancient Egyptians used to construct their boats many centuries ago. The modern model shipwright will learn how to select the finest wood, the best tools, and replicate the paints and colors favored by the ancient Egyptians. Also described is how to make the beautiful royal sail using freehand painting techniques, and how to make the miniature hieroglyphic symbols for each model.

GENERAL INSTRUCTIONS

These instructions relate to all three model-building projects, even though many centuries separate each pharaoh's reign. As stated previously, the projects are rated at a beginner's skill level. However, it is recommended that adult supervision be present when children under the age of twelve are using cutting tools.

WORKPLACE

The model builder should have a solid, well-lighted worktable for this project. You will also need a good-quality cutting mat and a flexible steel ruler in order to make safe and accurate pattern cuts using an X-ACTO knife. Many of these materials can be easily obtained at craft, hobby, and office supply stores.

SUPPLIES AND CONSTRUCTION MATERIALS

- Brushes, small bristle camel's hair (very fine, fine, ⅛", and ¼")
- Card stock
- Felt-tip pens, extra-fine point (green, red, medium brown, brown)
- Glue, white carpenter's
- Instant adhesive
- Magnifying glass (3" round)
- Masking tape
- Paint (water-based acrylic) in the following colors:

Black	Green
Black, flat	Green, dark
Blue	Green, light
Blue, light	Red
Blue, medium	Red, dark
Blue, navy	Red, medium
Brown	Tan
Brown, light	White
Flesh tone	White, bright
Gold leaf	Yellow

- Paper towels
- Pencil (#2)
- Rods (round brass) in the following sizes:

0.003"	0.012"
0.005"	0.016"
0.006"	0.020"
0.008"	0.030"
0.010"	

- Sandpaper, extra-fine (2 sheets)
- Steel wool (#000 grade)
- Varnish (clear water-based satin)
- White cotton string
- Wood sealer, clear
- Wood stain (light reddish brown, light oak)

PROJECT TOOLS

- Coping saw
- Drill with ⅛", ⅛", ¹⁄₁₆", ¹⁄₃₂", ¹⁄₆₄", ⅜" bits
- Modeling clamps, plastic (8)
- Needle-nose pliers, small
- Scissors
- Sewing needle (medium)
- Tweezers, small
- Wire cutter, small
- X-ACTO knife with extra blades

SAIL MATERIAL

Two sheets of either light colored papyrus paper or top-grade beige parchment paper. (NOTE: Inexpensive papyrus paper can be obtained from importers listed on the Internet.)

WOOD

- (Two sheets) 2" x 12" x ¹⁄₃₂" balsa wood
- (Two sheets) 2" x 12" x ¹⁄₁₆" balsa wood
- (Two sheets) 2" x 12" x ⅛" balsa wood
- (One sheet) 2" x 12" x ⅜" balsa wood
- (One) 12" x ¹⁄₁₆" round dowel
- (One) 12" x ⅛" round dowel
- (One) ¼" thick sheet of balsa, mahogany, walnut, basswood, apple, pecan, pear, red oak, or ash (for the base stand)

How to Make the Royal Sail

There are only two things necessary for you to do in order to make the pharaoh's sail. The first requires tracing the pattern in the book onto either the papyrus sheet or the parchment paper. The second is to paint the outline of the images on the papyrus or parchment.

It should be noted that each pharaoh's sail design and coloring is different. The reason for this is that the art style did change over the centuries separating these great pharaohs. This book provides the necessary patterns and easy-to-follow instructions on how to create each sail in Parts 1, 2, and 3.

To transfer the design onto the sail material, place the sail pattern under the blank sail sheet and gently trace the outline on the papyrus or parchment using a #2 pencil. Then go over the pencil markings with a medium brown, extra-fine point, felt-tip pen. Then paint the sail following the color guide provided for each sail using the water-based acrylic paints listed under Supplies and Construction Materials on page 2. This part of making the sail is fun. You will find that acrylic paint is easy to work with when reproducing the pharaoh's likeness and royal cartouches. Another great thing about acrylic paint is when it is dry the colors will closely resemble the heavily leaded paint used by ancient Egyptian artists.

Reproducing the Hieroglyphic Symbols, Canopy Designs, and Other Color Images

To reproduce the color designs you can make them yourself using extra-fine point felt-tip pens. The colors you will need are green, red, and brown. Or, you can easily cut out these decorative accents located on the inside covers. It will be your choice. Apply a light coat of clear water-based satin varnish to the paper to protect the designs and to give it an aged appearance.

Making the Patterns

Each boat has two pattern pages. Remove these pages from the book, and then glue them onto card stock. Carefully cut out the patterns using an X-ACTO knife. Having the patterns on card stock will make them easier to handle when tracing the patterns onto the wood. Each of the patterns has an initial on them for easy identification: K is for King Khufu's boat, H is for Queen Hatshepsut's boat, and R is for King Ramses II's boat.

Problem Solving

A first-time modeler should find these directions fun and easy to follow. However, if you do experience problems at any point during the construction, the important thing to remember is not to become discouraged. Ship modeling in general, and building ancient Egyptian royal boats in particular, is a very subjective artistic project. Just as the ancient model builders put their own artistic identity into their boats, so, too, will the modern boat builder bring their own unique artistic expression to the project. It is an interesting fact that archaeologists don't all agree on how a particular pharaoh's sailing boat would have appeared in real life since to date none have been discovered intact. So, you cannot make a mistake as far as the final appearance of the boat is concerned. It is your project to have fun with, so go for it!

THE HISTORY OF THE ANCIENT EGYPTIAN BOAT MODEL

The ancient Egyptians were the world's first serious model makers. Their civilization spanned almost five thousand years. For most of that period they constructed wonderful models of things and places from everyday life out of wood and clay. Most impressive are their miniature models of farm scenes with cattle and sheep and the shops of carpenters, weavers, potters, butchers, and bakers. The most common models the Egyptians made were boats. Today, in museums and private collections throughout the world, thousands of these historic artifacts are on display. Many of the models were lovingly constructed as toys for their children two thousand years before the birth of Christ.

The boat model was also valued in Egyptian culture as a religious symbol. They believed the soul, upon leaving the body, would then journey on a boat to heaven. It was in accordance with this hope that the dead person's family would place a model of a boat in the burial place so the soul would find its way to heaven. These Egyptian model boats were known as funerary models.

The finest funerary boat models were discovered in Egypt, and the most valuable are the ones belonging to King Tutankhamen (ruled 1361–1352 B.C). These boat models are 3' long and made of acacia wood and ivory. Even after thirty-five centuries, these models still retain their colorful decorations and fine linen sails. They are classic examples of Egyptian maritime art and technology.

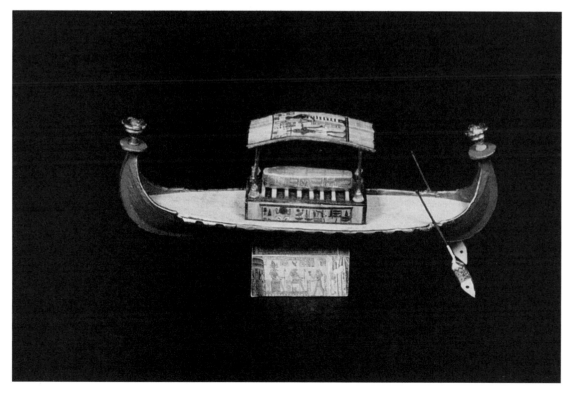

A PHARAOH'S FUNERARY BOAT (CA. 1900 B.C.)

PART 1

KING KHUFU'S ROYAL SAILING BOAT

A Brief History of King Khufu and the Shipbuilding Techniques (ca. 2500 b.c.)

King Khufu, who reigned from approximately 2551 to 2528 b.c., was a 4th Dynasty pharaoh who was best known for building the Great Pyramid of Giza in Egypt. He organized the construction of the pyramid, but not much else is known about Khufu's life due to the fact his tomb was robbed soon after his death. No remains of his mummy have ever been found, only the empty sarcophagus that lies in the center of the king's chamber inside the pyramid. Khufu's Great Pyramid is the only remaining Wonder of the Ancient World standing to this day. All that remains of this once powerful pharaoh is a nine-millimeter ivory statuette of him that was discovered at Abydos, Egypt. He is considered by many historians to be one of the great pharaohs of Egypt.

During Khufu's time there were many types of boats traveling along the Nile River. The most common boats were made from lightweight papyrus reeds. They were used for personal transport, light commerce, fishing, hunting, and, of course, warfare.

Larger boats like a pharaoh's sailing boat were made from native acacia wood and imported cedar from what is now the country of Lebanon. Cedar was very important to the Egyptians as a boat building material. Khufu's royal boat was built of relatively short blocks of timber that were braced and secured with strong rope made of halfa grass, wooden dowels, and copper staples. In addition, the boat might have had a large square sail made of thick coarse canvas gloriously painted with Khufu's likeness standing with the God Osiris, or perhaps the Goddess Mut. King Khufu probably used his boat for important state and religious functions and also excursions on the Nile with his wives, concubines, and children.

How to Make the Royal Boat's Sail

(1) Take a 7¾″ x 11¾″ sheet of light colored papyrus or a sheet of beige parchment paper and, using an X-ACTO knife, carefully cut out a 5⅝″ x 4⅜″ piece from the blank sheet. The sail's 5⅝″ side will be the length; the sail's 4⅜″ side will be the width. It is recommended that you cut out an extra piece to use as a practice piece for the painting of the sail.

(2) Place the 5⅝″ x 4⅜″ sheet squarely over the outline guide on page 11. Use a #2 pencil to gently trace the image onto the sail material. The image may appear light now, but once it is placed under a good light source the lines will be easily seen for the final tracing before the actual painting of the sail.

(3) Once the outline has been traced, gently retrace the pharaoh's image using a medium brown, extra-fine point, felt-tip pen so all the lines and hieroglyphs will stand out for the painting phase. If mistakes are made here in this process, use the spare sail material to start over again.

(4) Place the outlined papyrus or parchment paper on a clean sheet of unlined paper or on a clean cutting mat. Secure the edges of the sail material with thin strips of masking tape so the sail will not move during the painting and drying phase.

(5) Refer to the painting instructions on page 11 and the color photograph of the completed sail located on the inside front cover as a guide for what colors to use in the painting.

The paints are water-based acrylic and can be easily removed with water. For best results use small bristle camel's hair brushes: very fine, fine, ⅛″, and ¼″.

Begin by painting the outlines carefully with short, steady strokes using the ⅛″ brush with just a small amount of paint each time. Use a paper towel to clean off any excess paint from the brush. Once the outlines are painted, allow them to dry thoroughly before using the very fine and fine brushes to paint the small details like the facial features and costumes.

Once you are satisfied that all the details on the pharaoh's portrait and the hieroglyphic writing are complete, allow the paint to dry for two hours before applying a light coat of clear water-based satin varnish to both sides of the sail. The varnish will protect the paint and sail material from being damaged while handling and mounting the sail to the model's yardarm and mast.

The sail is now ready for mounting. Place the sail to the side for now while the next phase of construction begins.

MAKING THE HULL, MAIN DECK, BI-POLE MAST, YARDARM, AND THRONE PLATFORM

Refer to the patterns on pages 23 and 25, and the drawings on pages 19, 20, and 21 before starting this portion of the project. Begin by making the hull, then continue with the main deck, bi-pole mast, yardarm, and finally the throne platform—in that order.

All of the patterns are labeled for you on pages 23 and 25. Trace the patterns onto whatever wood you want: balsa, mahogany, walnut, etc. The wood should be a ³⁄₁₆″ thick sheet. Carefully use an X-ACTO knife to cut the patterns out. The hull is made sandwich style. (See the drawing on page 19 as a guide.) Starting with the left side of the boat's keel (using white carpenter's glue): glue number 1 to the boat's keel at the top. Next, glue number 2 to number 1, then glue number 3 to number 2, then, finally, glue number 4 to number 3. Use the curved deck as a reference when joining the sections together. The right side of the hull is built in the same manner as the left side: number 5 is glued to the boat's keel. Next, glue number 6 to number 5, then glue number 7 to number 6, then, finally, glue number 8 to number 7. Next, glue the main deck to the top of the hull. Secure them together with plastic modeling clamps. Allow these pieces to dry thoroughly. The hull is now ready for light sanding. Use a sheet of extra-fine sandpaper to gently smooth the hull's sharp edges ONLY. The hull should have a layered, or a stepped appearance. The pharaoh's boat hull should not have a smooth look.

The mast is a bi-pole, the style that was common 2,500 years before Christ. Made of red cedar, it was very strong in order to support the heavy coarse linen sail. The model's mast is made of two pieces of ⅛″ square wood strips that are slightly tapered at the top. The bi-pole mast is 5½″ long and is supported by three, ¹⁄₁₆″ thick strips. See the scale drawing of the mast on page 21 for the correct size and placement of these structural crossbeams. The bi-pole mast footing base is made from ¹⁄₁₆″ thick balsa wood measuring ⁹⁄₁₆″ long x ⅜″ wide. The top piece for the footing measures ¼″ x ¼″ x ¼″. Glue the pieces together in a stack. Refer to the drawing on page 20 for the correct placement of the mast-footing base on the main deck. The yardarm is made of a single piece of ¹⁄₁₆″ wood dowel. Follow the scale drawing on page 21 to make this piece.

The pharaoh's throne platform can be made from balsa, walnut, or basswood. The measurements are: ⁵⁄₁₆″ x 1½″ x 1⅛″. Use a piece of extra-fine sandpaper to remove any rough edges after cutting. Once this has been done, go to page 21 and cut out and color the four hieroglyphic strips. The four strips are to be glued to each side of the platform, or you can make and color your own hieroglyphic markings. Page 23 shows exactly where to glue the completed throne platform to the main deck. There is also a period floor design for the throne platform on page 21 (this is optional). Once all of these parts have been made, set them aside for assembly later.

OUTLINE GUIDE AND PAINTING INSTRUCTIONS
FOR KING KHUFU'S SAIL

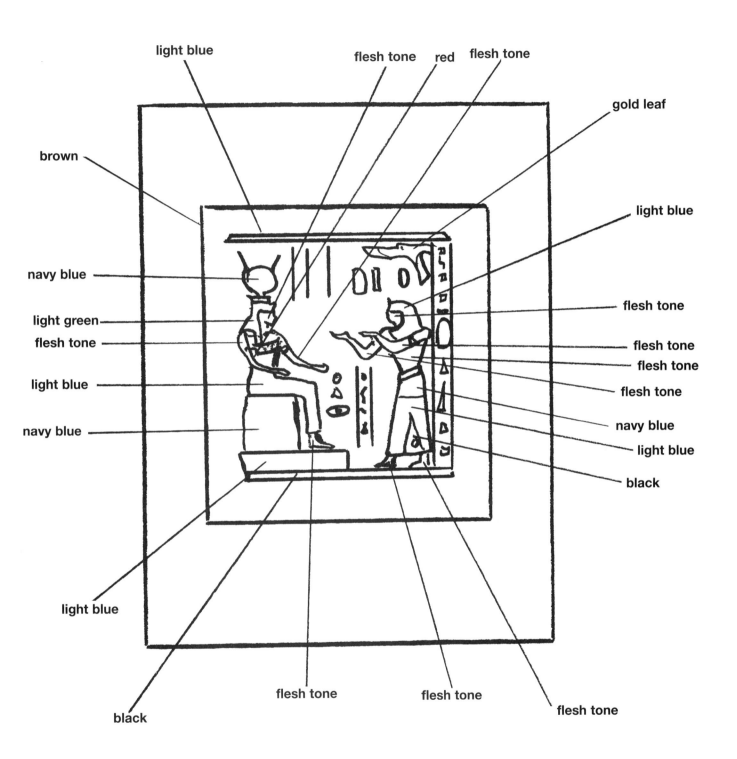

MAKING THE CANOPY,
FOUR STEERING OARS, EIGHT ROWING OARS,
AND DISPLAY STAND

It is best to use a ¹⁄₁₆″ thick sheet of balsa wood, because balsa can be easily curved when wet and it can hold that curve once it is dry. The canopy on page 19 shows that it has a slight fore and aft curve. This matches the boat's curve and will allow for easy mounting later to the deck. Trace the canopy's outline (see page 23) onto the balsa wood and carefully use an X-ACTO knife to cut it out. Use extra-fine sandpaper to lightly smooth the edges for a uniform appearance. Cut out and color the period painting of Goddess Mut on page 20 and glue it to the top of the canopy using a light film of white carpenter's glue (optional). Make five canopy support posts from 0.012″ round brass rods. Each post will be 1¼″ long.

The four steering oars are to be mounted onto the boat's stern with steering oar supports. (See page 23 for this pattern.) You will need to drill two ¹⁄₁₆″ holes in each support where indicated. The blades are made from $\frac{1}{16}$" thick balsa wood and each oar shaft is made of 0.008" round brass rods that are $1\frac{3}{8}$" long.

The eight rowing oars are attached to the main deck with eyelets. To make the eyelets carefully bend a 0.006" round brass rod into a small loop using needle-nose pliers. Make sure the loop is wide enough to hold each oar in place. The oar supports should be $\frac{3}{4}$" long. To install the oar supports, use a medium-size sewing needle to make the holes $\frac{1}{8}$" deep into the deck. Follow the scale drawing on page 20 for placement. To attach the oar supports to the deck, place a small drop of instant adhesive to the straight side of the eyelet and insert it into the hole. Hold it in place until it bonds. Repeat this until you have attached all of the oar supports to the deck. The blades are made from $\frac{1}{32}$" thick balsa wood and each oar shaft is made of 0.005" round brass rods that are $2\frac{1}{4}$" long. See page 20 for the shape of the blades. Apply a small drop of instant adhesive to the edge of the oar blade and carefully place the shaft onto the blade and hold until secure. Repeat this process until you have joined all of the oar blades to the oar shafts.

A scale drawing of the model's display stand and a copy of a 2500 B.C. pottery shard unique to the period of King Khufu can be found on page 22. Here you will see the shape of the $\frac{1}{4}$" high wood stand, as well as the shape and appearance of the ancient pottery shard image. This special piece will be mounted on the stand later. You will need to drill a $\frac{3}{8}$" hole into the stand where indicated. The base's mounting post that supports the completed model is a 0.016" round brass rod that is 2" long.

STAINING AND PAINTING THE CONSTRUCTED MODEL PARTS

The large Nile River boats during the time of King Khufu were mainly built of durable red cedar from the land that is now Lebanon. The natural color of these boats would have appeared a light brown or a slightly reddish brown depending on the age and dryness of the cedar before construction. The ancient Egyptians also used cedar to make the boat's mast, the yards for the sail, and the canopy. Therefore, these important pieces would also have the same color appearance as the hull.

The next step is the staining and hand painting of the previously constructed model parts, prior to their addition to the model's hull. If balsa wood was used to construct the model, then staining the hull and other wood parts will be necessary to achieve the correct color tone. First, apply a coat of clear wood sealer to all wood parts, including the hull, to get a uniform application of the wood stain when it is applied later. When the sealer is dry, use a light reddish brown stain on the hull and all other pre-finished wood parts. When the stain is dry, wipe off any excess stain with a clean paper towel before continuing.

If the model was constructed using a naturally dark wood such as mahogany, walnut, or pecan, then sealing and staining is not necessary as these woods already come very close to the correct color tone.

The painting of the four steering oars and eight rowing oars are next. Paint the shafts of the oars medium red. The four steering oar blades and the eight rowing oar blades are painted tan. See pages 19 and 20 for blade decoration ideas. (NOTE: These decorations are optional.) Once all the model parts have been painted or stained set them aside. The model's display stand is the next item for construction.

On page 22 you will find a full-scale pattern for the model's display stand. You may also create your own design for the base if you choose. Using your imagination to create new ideas is what makes scratch building models such a great and interesting lifetime hobby. If you choose to use the book's pattern, it is best to use a hardwood such as walnut or pear. This is because these woods have a beautiful color tone when sanded lightly and sealed with a quality satin varnish. See page 22 for the placement of the brass support to properly balance the completed model.

ASSEMBLING THE MODEL

Now that you have built all the parts for the model the next step is gluing them to the hull. Use white carpenter's glue for securing wood to wood and use instant adhesive to bond wood to metal or metal to metal. Using the diagrams as a guide (pages 19 and 20), glue the following parts to the hull in this order. Allow all parts to dry before continuing to the next piece.

BI-POLE MAST: Refer to page 20 for the location of the bi-pole mast footing on the main deck. Glue the footing into place, using white carpenter's glue, and let dry. Then place a drop of glue on both pieces of the mast's bottom and mount the mast onto the footing. Hold it steady for a moment until the glue bonds.

THRONE PLATFORM: Spread a thin film of white carpenter's glue on the platform's underside and secure it to the main deck and let it dry. See page 23 for the location of the throne platform on the main deck.

BRASS CANOPY SUPPORT POSTS: Drill five ½" holes, ⅛" deep into the main deck as shown on page 19. Apply a small drop of instant adhesive on each post bottom and insert the posts into the holes.

SUPPORTS FOR THE EIGHT ROWING OARS: The drawing on page 20 shows the location of the supports. Drill eight ¼₄" holes, ⅛" deep into the main deck. Then place a small drop of instant adhesive over each hole and insert the oar support eyelets into place.

PLACING EIGHT ROWING OARS INTO THE SUPPORTS: Insert the eight oars into the eyelet supports. Using instant adhesive, glue each oar to its support ensuring the oar is bonded well before continuing on. All eight oars should line up together when you have completed this section.

FOUR STEERING OARS: See the drawing on page 19 for the positioning of these oars. Insert the oars into the previously drilled holes in the supports and secure each oar with a small drop of instant adhesive. Hold each oar steady until the glue holds.

CANOPY: Apply a drop of instant adhesive to the top of each support post and then lay the canopy piece directly on the posts. Make sure the canopy is straight and square on the posts. Press the canopy down gently against the posts for a few moments until the glue holds.

YARDARM: Refer to page 21 for the exact location of the yardarm on the mast and then attach it to the mast with white carpenter's glue. Make sure that it is centered on the mast and you use enough glue so it bonds tight.

ROYAL SAIL: Apply a thin bead of white carpenter's glue along the leading edge of the yardarm. Then carefully place the top edge of the sail against the yardarm. Allow one hour to dry before continuing.

MOUNTING THE MODEL TO THE DISPLAY STAND: Place the bottom of the hull squarely over the base's support rod and gently press the model down with enough pressure to cause a dent to appear in the hull's bottom. Use a ⅛" drill to make one hole ¼" deep in the hull's bottom where the dent appears. Place a drop of instant adhesive in the hole and insert the support rod into the hole. Make sure the model is level and hold it secure until the glue firmly holds. Glue the pottery shard image to a ⅛" thick piece of balsa wood and attach to the display stand (optional).

SECURING THE ROPE RIGGING: Cut two pieces of white cotton string 3" long. Apply a drop of white carpenter's glue to the end of the string and place it against a top corner of the sail and allow it to dry thoroughly. Do this for both top corners of the sail. The other ends are then attached to the model by wrapping them around the left and right canopy posts and securing them with instant adhesive. Cut off any excess string.

Congratulations! Your model is now built and ready to display.

SCALE DRAWING OF THE HULL AND STEERING OARS (STARBOARD SIDE VIEW)

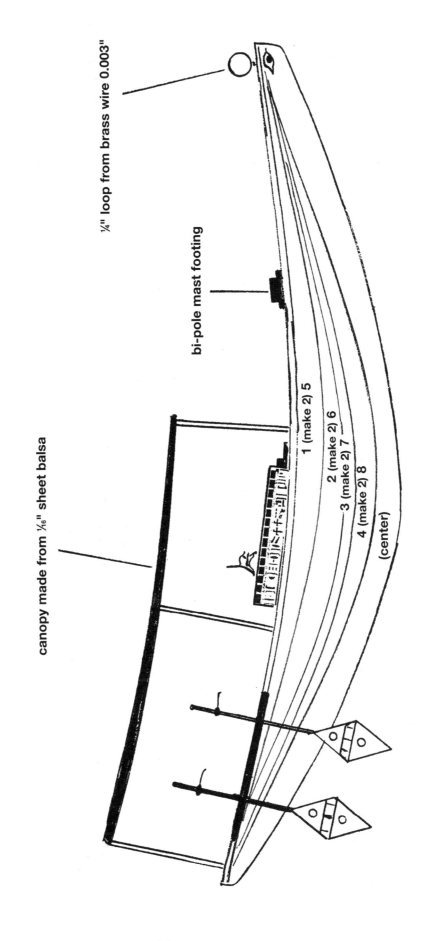

¼" loop from brass wire 0.003"

bi-pole mast footing

canopy made from ¹⁄₁₆" sheet balsa

1 (make 2) 5

2 (make 2) 6

3 (make 2) 7

4 (make 2) 8

(center)

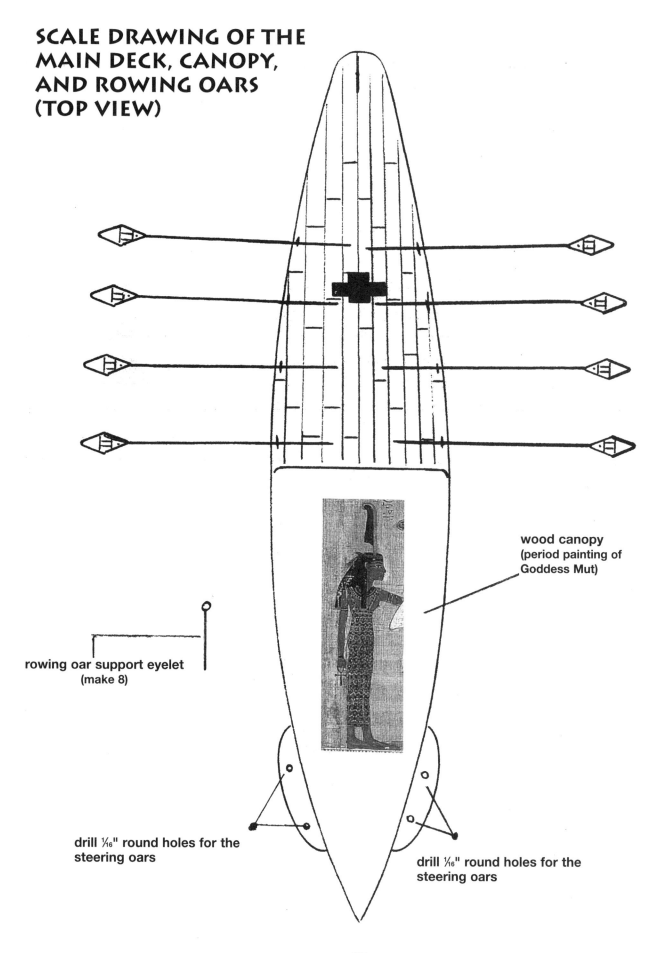

SCALE DRAWING OF THE MAIN DECK, CANOPY, AND ROWING OARS (TOP VIEW)

wood canopy
(period painting of
Goddess Mut)

rowing oar support eyelet
(make 8)

drill ¹⁄₁₆" round holes for the
steering oars

drill ¹⁄₁₆" round holes for the
steering oars

SCALE DRAWING OF THE BI-POLE MAST, THRONE PLATFORM, AND HIEROGLYPHICS

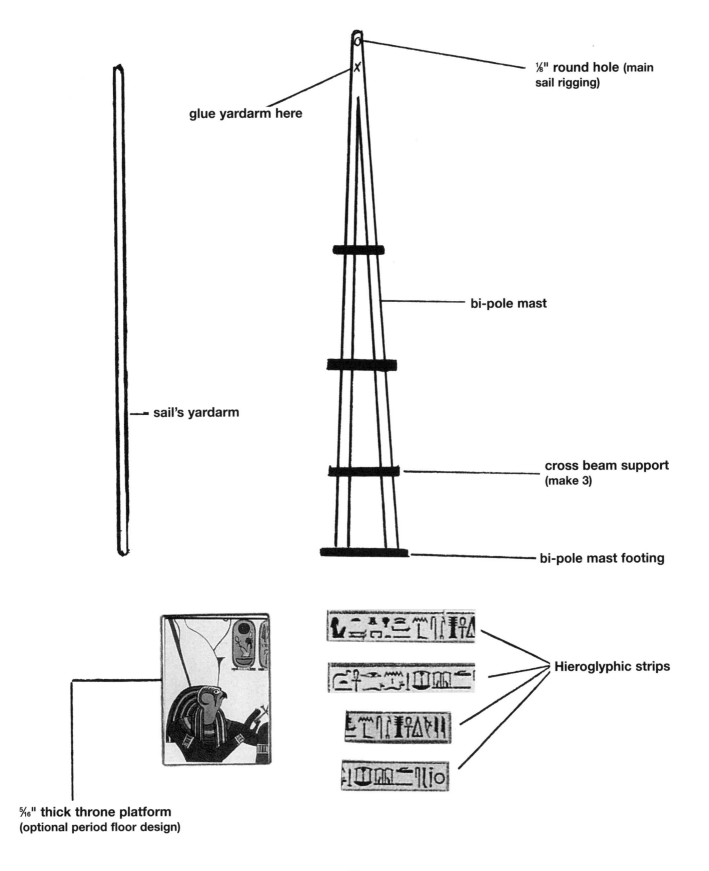

⅛" round hole (main sail rigging)

glue yardarm here

sail's yardarm

bi-pole mast

cross beam support (make 3)

bi-pole mast footing

Hieroglyphic strips

⁵⁄₁₆" thick throne platform (optional period floor design)

SCALE DRAWING OF THE MODEL'S BASE STAND AND POTTERY SHARD

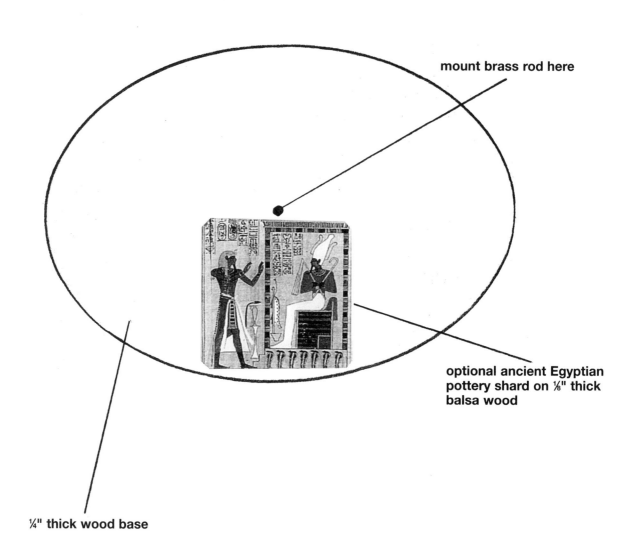

mount brass rod here

optional ancient Egyptian pottery shard on ⅛" thick balsa wood

¼" thick wood base

PATTERNS FOR THE MAIN DECK, CANOPY, KEEL, AND STEERING OAR SUPPORTS

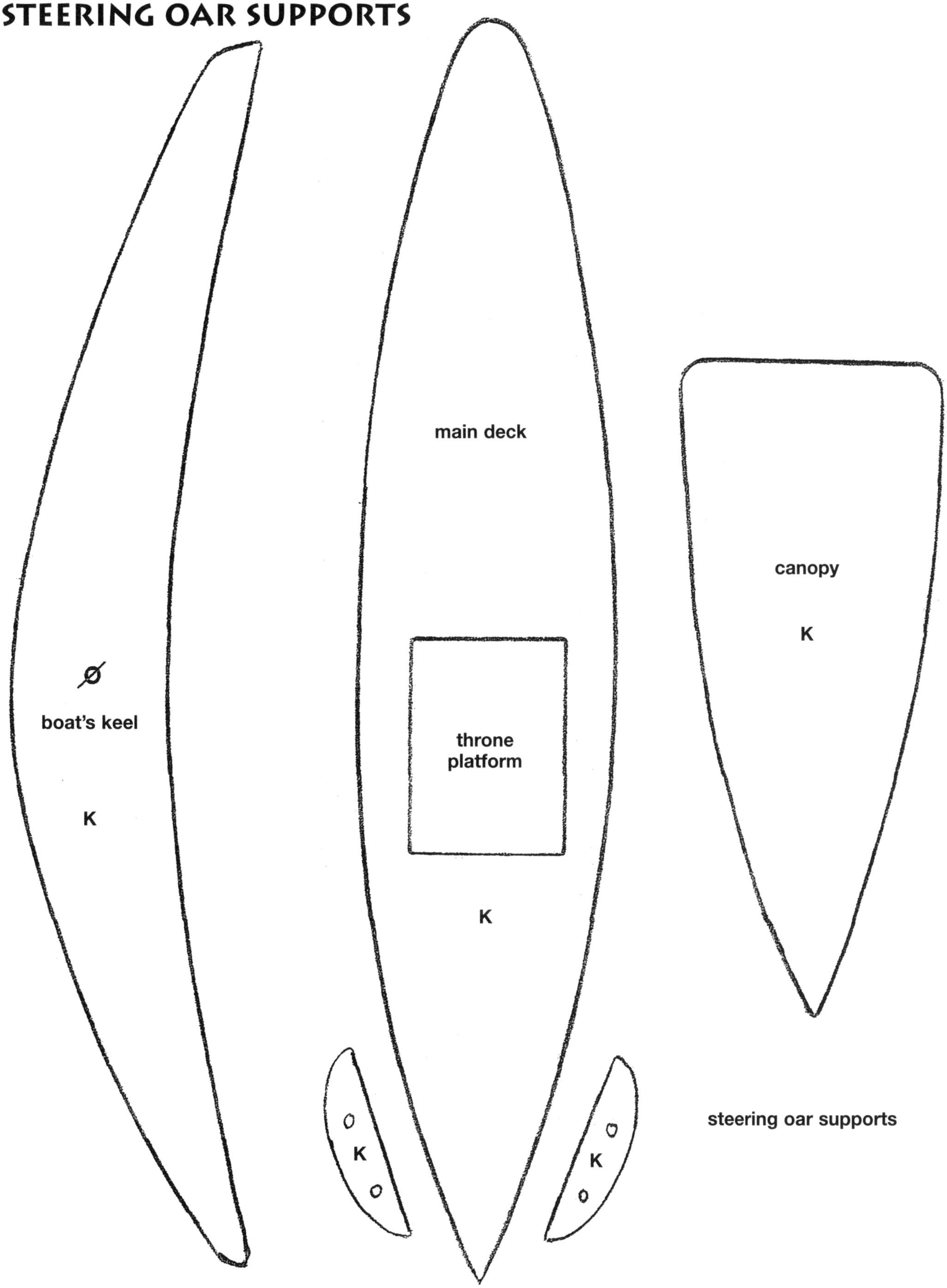

boat's keel

K

main deck

throne
platform

K

canopy

K

steering oar supports

K

K

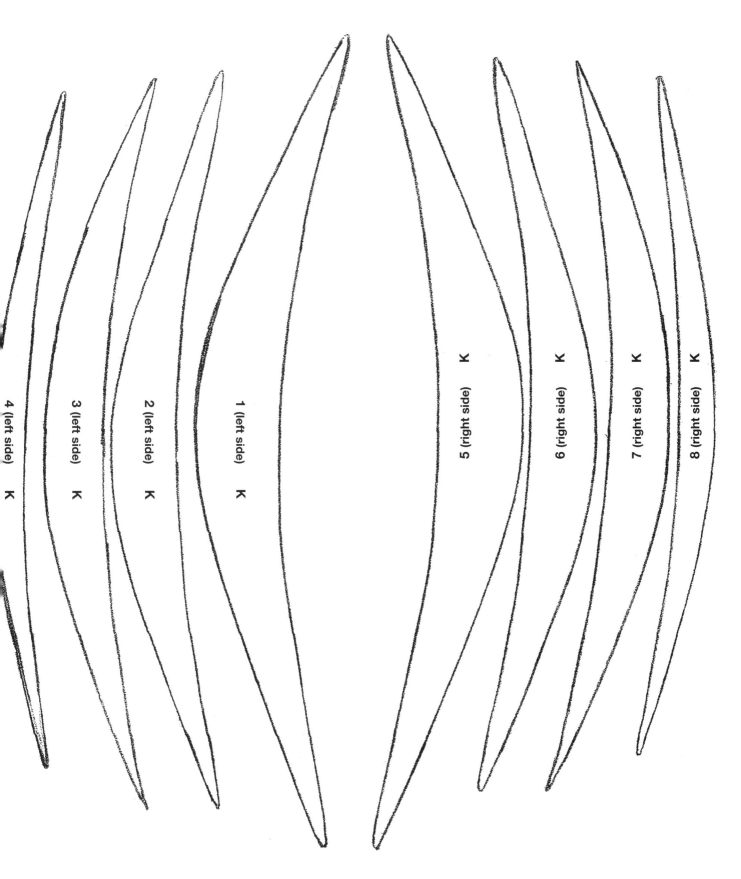

4 (left side)   K

3 (left side)   K

2 (left side)   K

1 (left side)   K

5 (right side)   K

6 (right side)   K

7 (right side)   K

8 (right side)   K

PART 2

QUEEN HATSHEPSUT'S ROYAL SAILING BOAT

A Brief History of Queen Hatshepsut and the Shipbuilding Techniques
(ca. 1467 b.c.)

Queen Hatshepsut reigned from approximately 1479 to 1458 b.c. and was the first great woman in recorded history. She was the fifth pharaoh of the 18th Dynasty of ancient Egypt. Queen Hatshepsut is regarded by Egyptologists as one of the most successful pharaohs, ruling longer than any female leader other than Cleopatra VII.

During her years in power, the Egyptian economy flourished and expanded through trade relations with neighboring countries. By making Egypt rich and powerful, Queen Hatshepsut brought about a Golden Age for art and technology that was to last long after her death. She was a pharaoh who created building projects that were grander and more numerous than any of her New Kingdom predecessors. During her reign many pieces of statuary were produced. These pieces can be found in almost every major museum in the world.

The shipbuilding technology of Egypt was very advanced during this time. Queen Hatshepsut's royal sailing boat was most likely state of the art in 1467 b.c., and constructed of the strongest woods available to shipwrights. Woods like sycamore from Nubia (what is now Sudan) and sturdy cedar imported from Lebanon were used to build the hull and mast. From their own land bordering the Nile River, shipwrights probably used the hardwood heart of the acacia tree to make the internal framing and supports very strong. Using these materials, Hatshepsut's boat was so well built and sturdy it didn't require the usual hogging ropes to support the vessel.

How to Make the Royal Boat's Sail

(1) Take a 7¾" x 11¾" sheet of light colored papyrus or a sheet of beige parchment paper and, using an X-ACTO knife, carefully cut out a 6" x 5" piece from the blank sheet. The sail's 6" side will be the length; the sail's 5" side will be the width. It is recommended that you cut out an extra piece to use as a practice piece for the painting of the sail.

(2) Place the 6" x 5" sheet squarely over the outline guide on page 31. Use a #2 pencil to gently trace the image onto the sail material. The image may appear light now, but once it is placed under a good light source the lines will be easily seen for the final tracing before the actual painting of the sail.

(3) Once the outline has been traced, gently retrace the pharaoh's image using a medium brown, extra-fine point, felt-tip pen so all the lines and hieroglyphics will stand out for the painting phase. If mistakes are made here in this process, use the spare sail material to start over again.

(4) Place the outlined papyrus or parchment paper on a clean sheet of unlined paper or on a clean cutting mat. Secure the edges of the sail material with thin strips of masking tape so the sail will not move during the painting and drying phase.

(5) Refer to the painting instructions on page 31 and the color photograph of the completed sail located on the inside back cover as a guide for what colors to use in the painting.

The paints are water-based acrylic and can be easily removed with water. For best results use small bristle camel's hair brushes: very fine, fine, ⅛", and ¼".

Begin by painting the outlines carefully with short, steady strokes using the ⅛" brush with just a small amount of paint each time. Use a paper towel to clean off any excess paint from the brush. Once the outlines are painted, allow them to dry thoroughly before using the very fine and fine brushes to paint the small details like the facial features and costumes.

Once you are satisfied that all the details on the pharaoh's portrait and hieroglyphic writing are complete, allow the paint to dry for two hours before applying a light coat of clear water-based satin varnish to both sides of the sail. The varnish will protect the paint and sail material from being damaged while handling and mounting the sail to the model's yardarm and mast.

The sail is now ready for mounting. Place the sail to the side for now while the next phase of construction begins.

Making the Hull, Main Deck, Mast, Yardarm, Throne Platform

Refer to the patterns on pages 43 and 45, and the drawings on pages 39, 40, and 41 before starting this portion of the project. Begin making the hull, then continue with the main deck, mast, the yardarm, and finally the throne platform—in that order.

All of the patterns are labeled for you on pages 43 and 45. Trace the patterns onto whatever wood you want: balsa, mahogany, walnut, etc. The wood should be a ³⁄₁₆″ thick sheet. Carefully use an X-ACTO knife to cut the patterns out. The hull is made sandwich style. (See the drawing on page 39 as a guide.) Starting with the right side of the main keel (using white carpenter's glue): glue piece 1R to the main keel at the top. Next, glue piece 2R to 1R, then glue piece 3R to 2R. Use the curved deck as a reference when joining the sections together. The right side of the hull is done. The left side of the hull is built in the same manner as the left side: piece 1L is glued to the main keel. Next, glue piece 2L to 1L, then, finally, glue piece 3L to 2L. Next, trace and cut out the main deck piece on page 45. Glue the deck piece to the top of the hull. Secure them together with plastic modeling clamps (see photo on page 33). Allow these pieces to dry thoroughly. The hull is now ready for light sanding. Use a sheet of extra-fine sandpaper to gently smooth the hull's sharp edges ONLY. The hull should have a layered, or a stepped appearance. The pharaoh's boat hull should not have a smooth look.

OUTLINE GUIDE AND PAINTING INSTRUCTIONS FOR QUEEN HATSHEPSUT'S SAIL

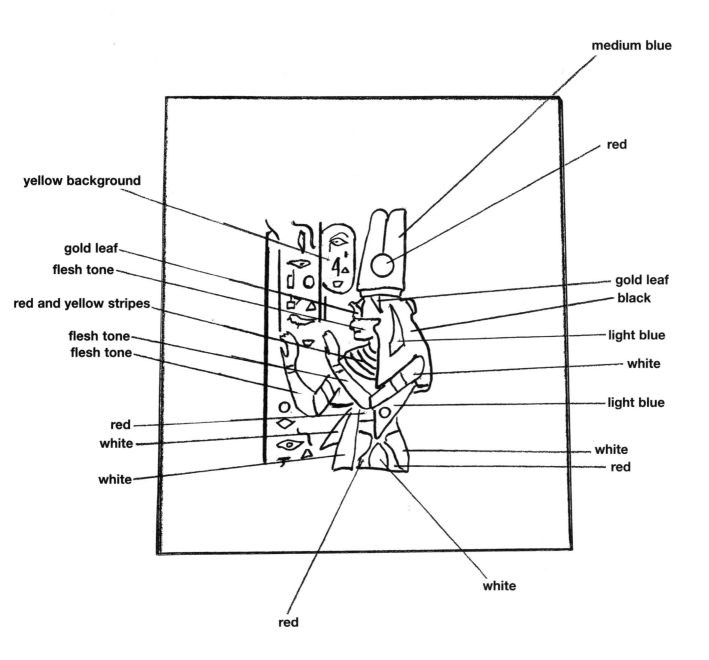

medium blue

red

yellow background

gold leaf

flesh tone

red and yellow stripes

flesh tone

flesh tone

gold leaf

black

light blue

white

light blue

red

white

white

white

red

white

red

Hieroglyphic writing is done by using green, red, and brown extra-fine point, felt-tip pens.

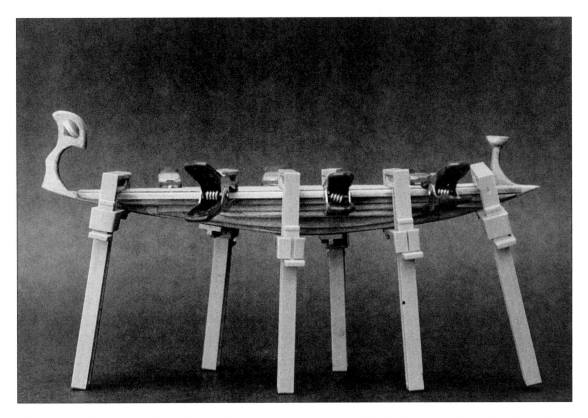

Refer to the scale drawing of the mast on page 41. This mast is a single pole, a style made popular during Queen Hatshepsut's time. The mast is 4½" long. See the drawing on page 41 for the general outline of the mast. Refer to the model drawing to locate the placement of the mast on page 40. The sail's top and bottom yards are made from 1⁄16" wood dowel. Follow the scale drawing on page 41 to make these pieces.

The pharaoh's throne platform can be made from balsa, walnut, or basswood. The measurements are: 1⁄8" x 7⁄8" x 7⁄8". The steps are three small 1⁄16" strips built up to resemble stairs. Use a piece of extra-fine sandpaper to remove any rough edges after cutting. Once this has been done, go to page 41 and cut out the hieroglyphic symbol strips. The strips are to be glued to each side of the platform, or you can make and color your own hieroglyphic markings. Page 40 shows exactly where to glue the completed throne platform to the main deck. There is also a period floor design for the throne platform on page 41 (this is optional). Once all of these parts have been made, set them aside for assembly later.

Making the Canopy,
Two Steering Oars, Six Rowing Oars,
and Display Stand

It is best to use a ¹⁄₁₆″ thick sheet of balsa wood, because balsa can be easily curved when wet and it can hold that curve once it is dry. The canopy pattern on page 39 shows that it has a wavelike appearance. To duplicate these curves after cutting out the canopy piece on page 45, hold the wood under warm water for a few minutes then gently bend and form the wood into a slight wavelike appearance. Make the four canopy support posts from 0.012″ round brass rods. Each post will be 1¼″ long.

The two steering oars are to be mounted onto the boat's stern with steering oar supports. (See page 45 for this pattern.) You will need to drill one ¹⁄₁₆″ hole in each support where indicated. The blades are made from ¹⁄₁₆″ thick balsa wood and each oar shaft is made of 0.008″ round brass rods that are 1″ long.

The six rowing oars are attached to the main deck with eyelets. To make the eyelets carefully bend a 0.006″ round brass rod into a small loop using needle-nose pliers. Make sure the loop is wide enough to hold each oar in place. The blades are made from ¹⁄₃₂″ thick balsa wood and each oar shaft is made of 0.005″ round brass rods that are 1½″ long.

A scale drawing of the model's display stand and a copy of a 1467 B.C. pottery shard from Queen Hatsheput's time period can be found on page 42. Here you will see the shape of the ¼″ high wood stand, as well as the shape and appearance of the ancient pottery shard image. This special piece will be mounted on the stand later. The base's mounting post that supports the completed model is made from a 0.016″ round brass rod that is 2″ long. Once this part of the project has been completed, set the pieces aside for assembly later.

STAINING AND PAINTING THE CONSTRUCTED MODEL PARTS

The medium-size Nile River boats like Queen Hatshepsut's were usually built of sycamore and cedar from the land that is now Lebanon. The natural color of these boats would have appeared a light reddish blond color depending on the age and dryness of both woods before construction. The ancient Egyptians also used cedar to make the boat's mast, yards for the sail, and the canopy. Therefore, these important pieces would also have the same color appearance as the hull.

The next step is the staining and hand painting of the previously constructed model parts, prior to their addition to model's hull. If balsa wood was used to construct the model, then staining the hull and other wood parts will be necessary to achieve the correct color tone. First, apply a coat of clear wood sealer to all wood parts, including the hull, to get a uniform application of the wood stain when it is applied later. When the sealer is dry, use a light oak stain on the hull and all other pre-finished wood parts. When the stain is dry, wipe off any excess stain with a clean paper towel before continuing.

If the model was constructed using a naturally light colored wood like basswood or pear, then sealing and staining may not be necessary as these woods come very close to the correct color tone.

The painting of the two oar supports, two steering oars, and six rowing oars are next. Paint the shafts and handles of the rowing oars dark red. The six rowing oar blades and the two steering oar blades are painted bright white. See page 41 for blade decoration ideas. (NOTE: These decorations are optional.) The six oar supports (see eyelets on page 40) are painted flat black. Once all the model parts have been painted or stained set them aside for now. The model's display stand is the next item for construction.

On page 42 you will find a full-scale pattern for the model's display stand. You may also create your own design for the base if you choose. Using your imagination to create new ideas is what makes scratch building models such a great and interesting lifetime hobby.

If you choose to use the book's pattern, it is best to use a hardwood such as oak or apple. This is because these woods have a beautiful color tone when sanded lightly and sealed with a quality satin varnish. See page 42 for the placement of the brass support to properly balance the completed model.

ASSEMBLING THE MODEL

Now that you have built all the parts for the model the next step is gluing them to the hull. Use white carpenter's glue for securing wood to wood and use instant adhesive to bond wood to metal or metal to metal. Using the diagrams as a guide (pages 39 and 40), glue the following parts to the hull in this order. Allow all parts to dry before continuing to the next piece.

MAST: Begin by drilling a ⅛" round hole, ¼" deep into the main deck for the mast. See page 40 for the location of the mast. Apply a drop of white carpenter's glue on the mast bottom and insert it into the hole. Hold it in place for a moment until the glue bonds.

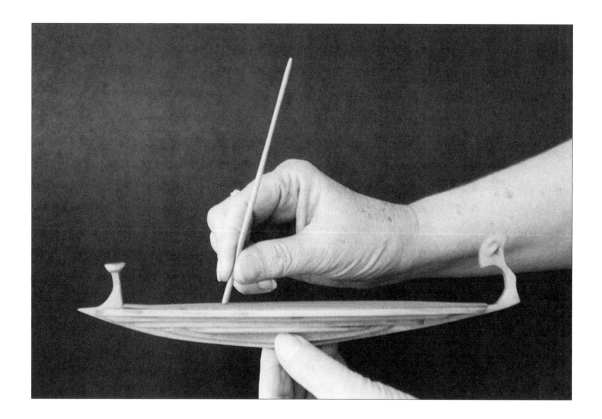

THRONE PLATFORM: Spread a thin film of white carpenter's glue on the platform's underside and secure it to the main deck and let it dry. See page 40 for the location of the throne platform on the main deck.

BRASS CANOPY SUPPORT POSTS: Drill four ½₂″ round holes, ⅛″ deep into the main deck as shown on page 39. Use a small drop of instant adhesive on each post and insert the posts into the holes.

SUPPORTS FOR THE SIX ROWING OARS: The drawing on page 45 shows the location of the supports. Drill six ¼₄″ holes, ⅛″ deep into the main deck. Then place a small drop of instant adhesive over each hole and insert the oar support eyelets into place.

PLACING SIX ROWING OARS INTO THE SUPPORTS: Insert the six oars into the eyelet supports. Using instant adhesive, glue each oar to its support ensuring the oar is bonded well before continuing on. All six oars should line up together when you have completed this section.

TWO STEERING OARS: Refer to the drawing of the steering oars on page 41 for the positioning of these oars. Insert the oars into the previously drilled holes and secure each oar with a drop of instant adhesive. Hold each oar steady until the glue holds.

CANOPY: Place a drop of instant adhesive to the top of each support post and then lay the canopy piece directly on the posts. Make sure the canopy is straight and square on the posts. Press the canopy down gently against the posts for a few moments until the glue holds.

YARDARM: Refer to page 41 for the exact location of the yardarm on the mast and then attach it to the mast with white carpenter's glue. Make sure that it is centered on the mast and you use enough glue so it bonds tight.

ROYAL SAIL: Apply a thin bead of white carpenter's glue along the leading edge of the yardarm. Then carefully place the top edge of the sail against the yardarm. Allow one hour to dry before continuing.

MOUNTING THE MODEL TO THE DISPLAY STAND: Place the bottom of the hull squarely over the base's support rod and gently press the model down with enough pressure to cause a dent to appear in the hull's bottom. Use a ⅛″ drill to make one hole ¼″ deep in the hull's bottom where the dent appears. Place a drop of instant adhesive in the hole and insert the support rod into the hole. Make sure the model is level and hold it secure until the glue firmly holds. Glue the pottery shard image to a ⅛″ thick piece of balsa wood and attach to the display stand (optional).

SECURING THE ROPE RIGGING: See page 27 for the placement of the rigging rope on the sail. Cut two pieces of white cotton string 10″ long and attach one end to the corner of the sail's bottom edge. Apply a drop of white carpenter's glue to the end of the string and place it against a corner of the sail and allow it to dry thoroughly. Do this for both corners of the sail. The other end is then attached to the model by wrapping it around the last rowing oar support and gluing it with instant adhesive. Cut of any excess string.

Congratulations! Your model is now built and ready for display.

SCALE DRAWING OF THE HULL, STEERING OARS, AND DECK (PORT SIDE VIEW)

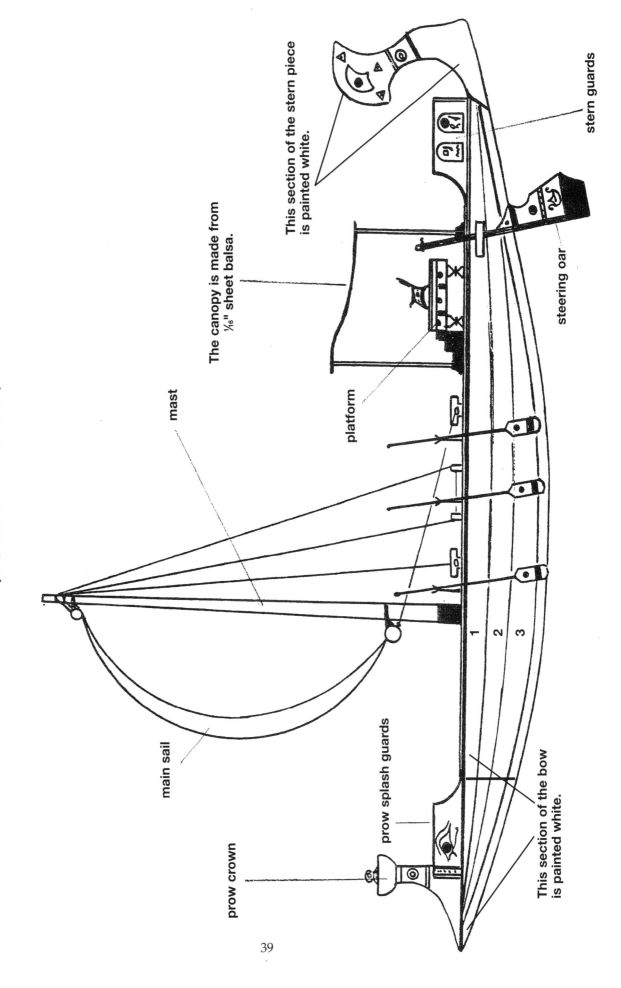

This section of the stern piece is painted white.

stern guards

The canopy is made from 1/16" sheet balsa.

steering oar

mast

platform

main sail

prow splash guards

prow crown

This section of the bow is painted white.

1

2

3

SCALE DRAWING OF THE MAIN DECK AND CANOPY (TOP VIEW)

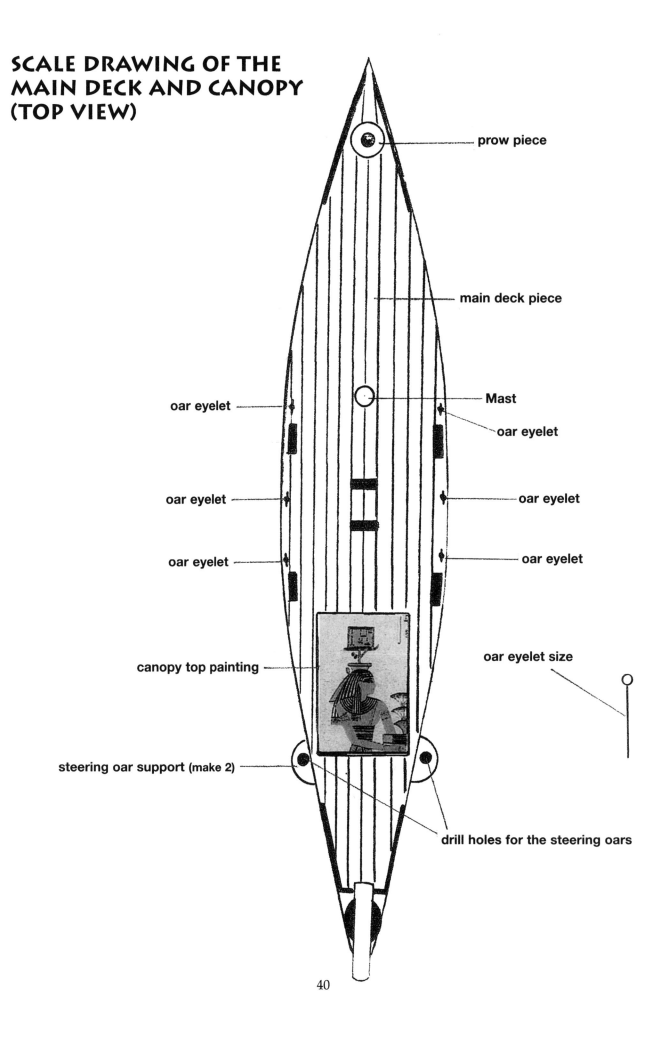

prow piece

main deck piece

oar eyelet

Mast

oar eyelet

oar eyelet

oar eyelet

oar eyelet

oar eyelet

oar eyelet size

canopy top painting

steering oar support (make 2)

drill holes for the steering oars

SCALE DRAWING OF THE MAST, YARDARM, THRONE PLATFORM, STEERING AND ROWING OARS, AND HIEROGLYPHICS

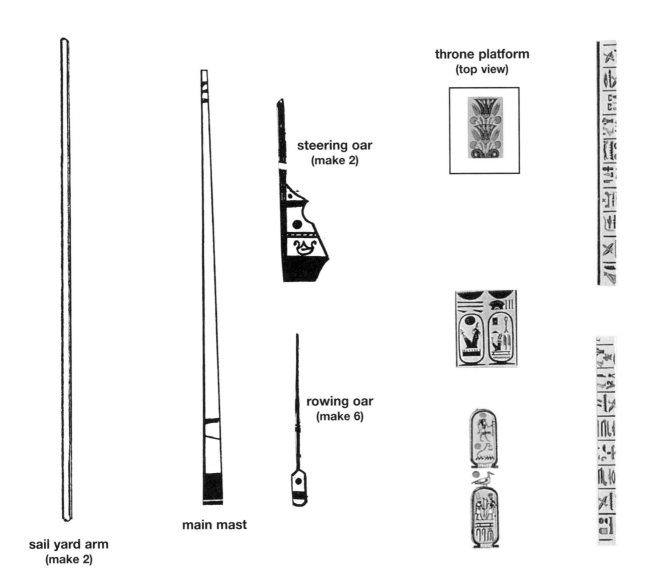

throne platform
(top view)

steering oar
(make 2)

rowing oar
(make 6)

main mast

sail yard arm
(make 2)

SCALE DRAWING OF THE MODEL'S BASE STAND AND POTTERY SHARD

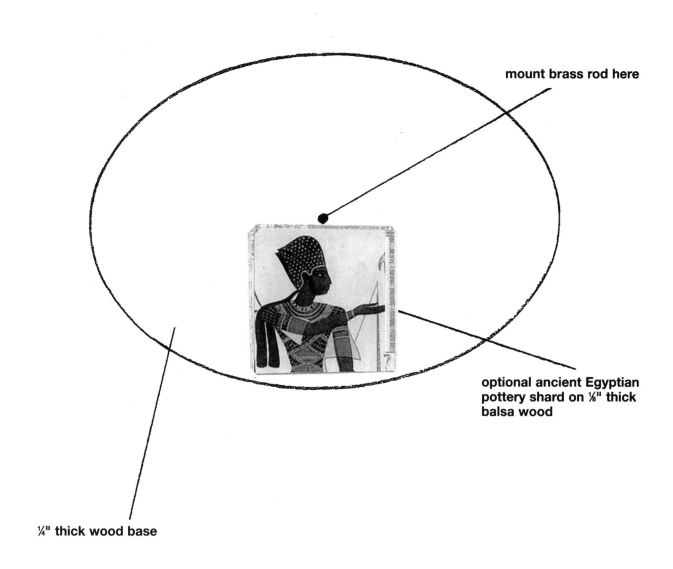

mount brass rod here

optional ancient Egyptian pottery shard on ⅛" thick balsa wood

¼" thick wood base

PATTERNS FOR THE HULL SECTIONS

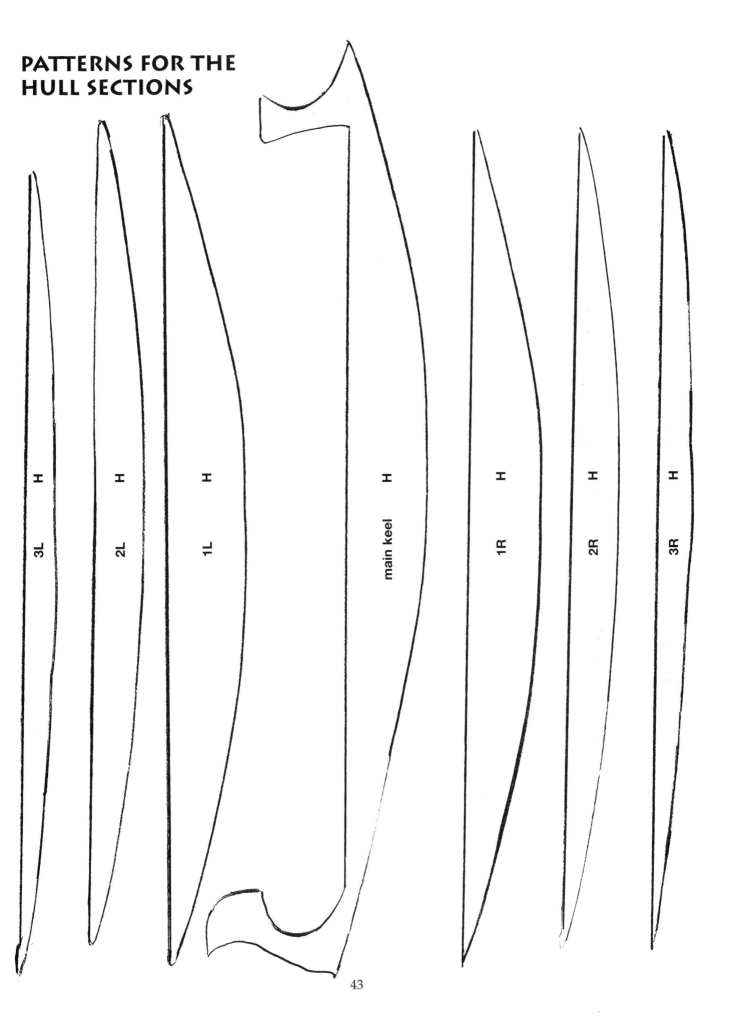

3L H

2L H

1L H

main keel H

1R H

2R H

3R H

43

PATTERNS FOR THE FORE STEM CAP, PLATFORM, STEERING OAR SUPPORTS, MAIN DECK, AND CANOPY

(H) fore stem cap

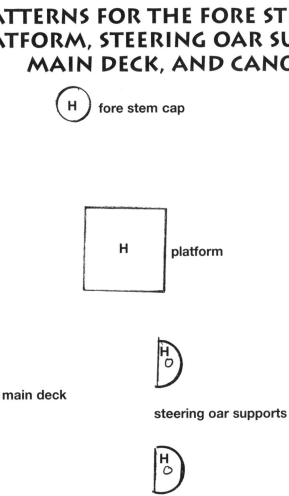

H platform

H
steering oar supports

H

main deck

canopy top piece

bow splash guard
(make 2)

stern guard
(make 2)

PART 3

KING RAMSES II's ROYAL SAILING BOAT

A Brief History of King Ramses II and the Shipbuilding Techniques (ca. 1250 b.c.)

The word pharaoh is not Egyptian in origin, but comes from the ancient Hebrew word for "leader." If ever a pharaoh epitomized that title it was Ramses II, an Egyptian king of the 19th Dynasty who reigned from 1279 to 1213 b.c. Greatly respected by his people and enemies alike, he was given the title "Ramses the Great" in his own lifetime.

Egyptologists believe it was Ramses II who was the pharaoh during the Jewish exodus from Egypt. His long active reign did cover that historic period in time. Ramses II lived during the time referred to as the Age of Classical Antiquity. He was a builder of cities and raised the standard of living for his subjects. He made Egypt a wealthy and powerful land whose influence spread from what is now called Sudan, Palestine, and Syria. Upon his death he was buried in the Valley of the Kings where, in 1881, his mummy was discovered in a simple grave. Today his remains are kept at the Cairo Museum.

As for the shipbuilding technology during this time, Ramses II built the largest warships for his navy than any of the previous rulers of Egypt. Today, the Cairo Museum has an impressive display of Ramses II's warships on exhibition. These wonderful models of the vessels in his once magnificent navy are on display only a few steps away from where Ramses II's mummy rests.

HOW TO MAKE THE ROYAL BOAT'S SAIL

(1) Take a 7¾" x 11¾" sheet of light colored papyrus or a sheet of beige parchment paper and, using an X-ACTO knife, carefully cut out a 4" x 3" piece from the blank sheet. The sail's 4" side will be the length; the sail's 3" side will be the width. It is recommended that you cut out an extra piece to use as a practice piece for the painting of the sail.

(2) Place the 4" x 3" sheet squarely over the outline guide on page 51. Use a #2 pencil to gently trace the image onto the sail material. The image may appear light now, but once it is placed under a good light source the lines will be easily seen for the final tracing before the actual painting of the sail.

(3) Once the outline has been traced, gently retrace the pharaoh's image using a medium brown, extra-fine point, felt-tip pen so all the lines and hieroglyphs will stand out for the painting phase. If mistakes are made here in this process, use the spare sail material to start over again.

(4) Place the outlined papyrus or parchment paper on a clean sheet of unlined paper or on a clean cutting mat. Secure the edges of the sail material with thin strips of masking tape so the sail will not move during the painting and drying phase.

(5) Refer to the painting instructions on page 51 and the color photograph of the completed sail located on the inside back cover as a guide for what colors to use in the painting.

The paints are water-based acrylic and can be easily removed with water. For best results use small bristle camel's hair brushes: very fine, fine, ⅛", and ¼".

Begin by painting the outlines carefully with short, steady strokes using the ⅛" brush with just a small amount of paint each time. Use a paper towel to clean off any excess paint from the brush. Once the outlines are painted, allow them to dry thoroughly before using the very fine and fine brushes to paint the small details like the facial features and costumes.

Once you are satisfied that all the details on the pharaoh's portrait and the hieroglyphic writing are complete, allow the paint to dry for two hours before applying a light coat of clear water-based satin varnish to both sides of the sail. The varnish will protect the paint and sail material from being damaged while handling and mounting the sail to the model's yardarm and mast.

The sail is now ready for mounting. Place the sail to the side for now while the next phase of construction begins.

Making the Hull, Main Deck, Mast, Yardarm, Rowing Oars, Steering Oars, Oar Supports, Cabin Cupolas, Prow Pieces, and Display Stand

Refer to the patterns on pages 59 and 61, and the drawings on pages 56 and 57 before starting this portion of the project. Begin making the hull, then continue with the main deck, mast, yardarm, rowing and steering oars, oar supports, both cabin cupolas, the prow guards, and, finally, the display stand.

All of the patterns are labeled for you on pages 59 and 61. Trace the patterns onto whatever wood you want: balsa, mahogany, etc. The wood should be a ³⁄₁₆″ thick sheet. Carefully use an X-ACTO knife to cut the patterns out. The hull is made sandwich style. (See the drawing on page 56 as a guide.) Starting with the left side of the boat's keel: glue number 1 to the boat's keel at the top, Next, glue number 2 to number 1, then, finally, glue number 3 to number 2. Use the curved deck as a reference when joining the sections together. The left side of the hull is done. The right side of the hull is built in the same manner as the left side: number 1 is glued to the boat's keel. Next, glue the number 2 to number 1, then, finally, glue number 3 to number 2. Allow these pieces to dry thoroughly. Next, glue the main deck to the top of the hull. Secure them together with plastic modeling clamps. The hull is now ready for light sanding. Use a sheet of extra-fine sandpaper to gently smooth the hull's sharp edges ONLY. The hull should have a layered, or a stepped appearance. The pharaoh's boat hull should not have a smooth look.

Construct the mast and yardarm from the patterns shown on page 59. Use an ⅛″ round dowel for the mast and ¹⁄₁₆″ round dowel for the yardarm. Use extra-fine sandpaper to shape the mast.

The next part of the project involves making the two large steering oars that will mount at the rear of the boat and the ten rowing oars (see photo on page 53). Refer to page 57 for these patterns. The steering oar blades are made from ¹⁄₁₆″ thick balsa wood. The shafts are 0.020″ round brass rods. The rowing oars blades are made from ¹⁄₃₂″ thick balsa wood with 0.010″ round brass rods for the shafts. The two steering oar supports are on page 59. Trace their patterns onto a ¹⁄₁₆″ thick sheet of basswood and carefully cut them out. Mark the holes where the steering oars will be inserted and drill a 0.020″ hole into each support. When the supports are completed, see page 57 for where to glue the port and starboard support.

OUTLINE GUIDE AND PAINTING INSTRUCTIONS
FOR RAMSES II'S SAIL

To color the hieroglyphic symbol writing use extra-fine point felt pens in the colors of brown, green, and red. (Alternate the colors for every symbol.)

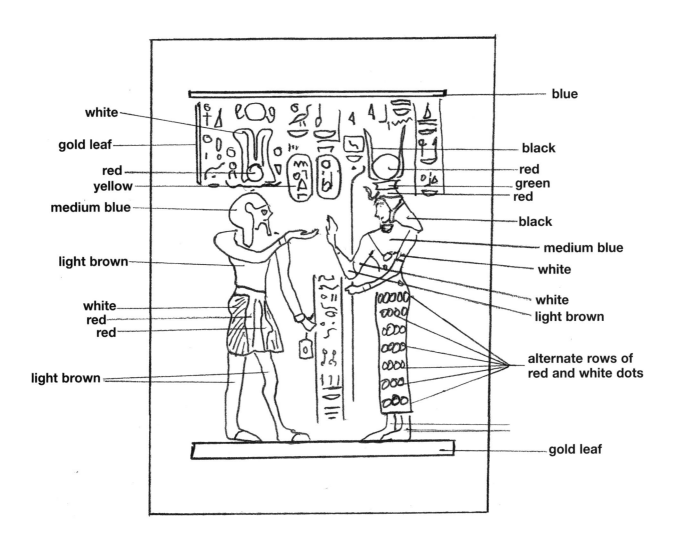

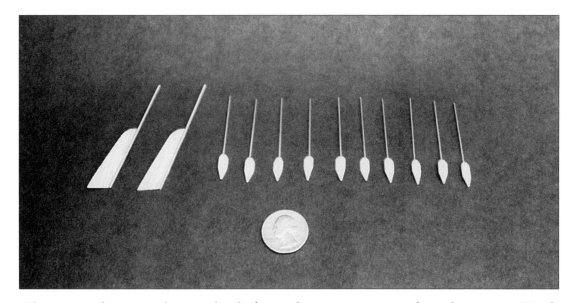

The two cabin cupolas are built from the same pattern found on page 59. On that page there are five pieces for the cupola (top, base, rear, and two sides). Trace the patterns for the base, rear, and two sides onto a ⅟₁₆″ thick sheet of basswood then cut out the pieces. Begin building the cupola by gluing the rear and two sides to the base. Allow these small and delicate parts to dry thoroughly. The four posts supporting the cabin top are made from ⅟₁₆″ round dowels. Refer to page 56 for the size of the two front and two rear posts. Glue the posts into position and when dry, trace the cabin top pattern on page 59 onto a ⅟₁₆″ sheet of balsa wood. Cut out the cabin top piece and soak it in warm water for a minute so it can be bent slightly to match the curve of the canopy on page 56. Bend the canopy piece and let it dry. Then glue it to the four posts. See page 56 for hieroglyphic symbols to be cut out, colored, and applied to the sides of the cupolas, and page 57 for a period painting for the cupola's top. (NOTE: These highly decorated cabin cupolas during the reign of Ramses II were strictly reserved for royalty.) Make two complete cabin cupolas. Also, notice on page 56 that the cabins face each other on the main deck.

The platform where the mast and sail are mounted is made from a ⅜″ thick piece of balsa wood 2″ long x ¾″ wide. The stairs leading up to the platform are made of ⅛″ thick balsa wood. See page 59 for these patterns.

The pattern for the two prow pieces is shown on page 59. Use ⅟₁₆″ thick balsa wood to make these pieces. The ancient Egyptian mariners considered the "Eye of Horus," a symbol of good luck. Draw these patterns onto your prow pieces using an extra-fine point, felt-tip pen. Once all these parts have been completed, set them aside for assembly later.

Constructing the display stand is next. Take a piece of ¼″ thick red oak and using the display stand pattern on page 58 trace that pattern onto the oak piece. Cut out the piece using a coping saw. Once this is done, sandpaper the oval shape smooth and seal the base with water-based satin varnish. The base's mounting post that supports the completed model is a 0.030″ round brass rod that is 2″ long.

THE STAINING AND PAINTING OF THE CONSTRUCTED MODEL PARTS

A large Nile River boat during the reign of King Ramses II was built of white cedar and acacia wood. The natural color of these boats would have appeared a light oak color. The color tone would have varied from vessel to vessel depending on the wood's age and dryness before construction. The ancient Egyptians also used white cedar to make the mast, yardarm, cabins, and oars. Therefore, it can be assumed that the color of these pieces would also have match the color of the hull.

If balsa wood was used to construct the model, then staining the hull and other wood parts will be necessary to achieve the correct color tone. First, apply a coat of clear wood sealer to all wood parts, including the hull, to get a uniform application of the wood stain when it is applied later. When the sealer is dry, use a light oak stain on the hull and all other pre-finished wood parts. When the stain is dry, wipe off any excess stain with a clean paper towel before continuing.

If the model was constructed using a slightly darker wood like pecan or light walnut, then sealing and staining is not necessary as these woods already come close to the correct tone for this boat.

The painting of the ten rowing oars and the two large steering oars is next. The shafts are painted dark green and the blade portion of each oar is painted white. See page 57 for oar blade decorations (optional).

ASSEMBLING THE MODEL

Now that you have built all the parts for the model the next step is gluing them to the hull. Use white carpenter's glue for securing wood to wood and use instant adhesive to bond wood to metal or metal to metal. Using the diagrams as a guide (pages 56 and 57), glue the following parts to the hull in this order. Allow all parts to dry before continuing to the next piece.

MAST: Begin by drilling a ⅛" hole, ¼" deep into the main deck for the mast. See page 56 for the location of the mast. Place a drop of white carpenter's glue on the mast bottom and insert the mast into the hole and allow it to dry.

PHARAOH'S PLATFORM: Refer to page 57 for the platform's location on the main deck. Spread a thin coat of white carpenter's glue on the platform bottom and secure it to the main deck.

CABIN CUPOLAS: Both cupolas are glued to the main deck. See page 56 for the location of the cupolas. (NOTE: The open sections of the cupolas face each other.) Only a small amount of white carpenter's glue is needed to secure the cupola to the deck. Allow at least 45 minutes for these pieces to dry.

TEN ROWING OAR SUPPORTS: Refer to page 47 for the location of the ten rowing oar supports (5 on each side). Drill ten ¼₄″ holes, ⅛″ deep into the main deck. Place a small drop of instant adhesive into the hole and insert the oar support. Keep each support even with respect to the other supports.

MOUNTING THE TWO LARGE STEERING OARS: See the drawing on page 56 for the positioning of these oars. Secure each oar to its support hole with a drop of instant adhesive and allow time for them to dry completely.

YARDARM: Center the yardarm at the top of the mast and use a drop or two of white carpenter's glue to secure it to the main mast. Allow a few minutes for the glue to set so it bonds tight.

ROYAL SAIL: Place a thin bead of white glue across the top part of the sail yardarm. Then carefully place the top of the sail flat against the yardarm and allow time to dry completely before continuing.

PLACING TEN ROWING OARS INTO THE SUPPORTS: Insert the ten oars into the eyelet supports. Using instant adhesive, glue each oar to its support ensuring the oar is bonded well before continuing on. All ten oars should line up together when you have completed this section.

SECURING THE STRING RIGGING TO THE SAIL AND MODEL: Refer to page 47 for the placement of the sail ropes and where to secure them. Cut two pieces of string 8″ long for the sail's rigging. Place a drop of white carpenter's glue on the bottom corners of the sail. Press one corner of the string onto the glue and allow it to dry. When dry, the free end of each string is wrapped around the last rowing oar post and secured using instant adhesive.

MOUNTING THE MODEL TO THE DISPLAY STAND: Place the bottom of the hull squarely over the base's support rod and gently press the model down with enough pressure to cause a dent to appear in the hull's bottom. Use a ⅛″ drill to make one hole ¼″ deep in the hull's bottom where the dent appears. Place a drop of instant adhesive in the hole and insert the support rod into the hole. Make sure the model is level and hold it secure until the glue firmly holds. Glue the pottery shard image to a ⅛″ thick piece of balsa wood and attach to the display stand (optional).

Congratulations! Your model is now built and ready to display.

SCALE DRAWING OF THE HULL, CABINS, PLATFORM, AND STEERING OARS
(PORT SIDE VIEW)

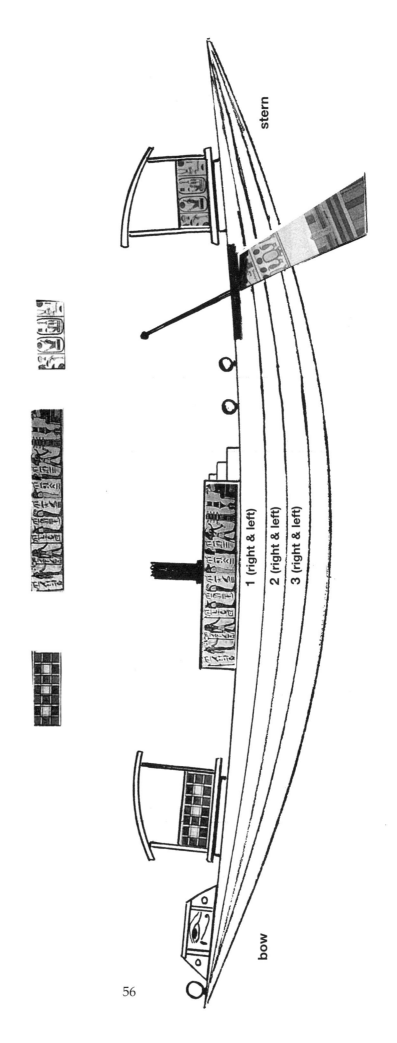

stern

1 (right & left)
2 (right & left)
3 (right & left)

bow

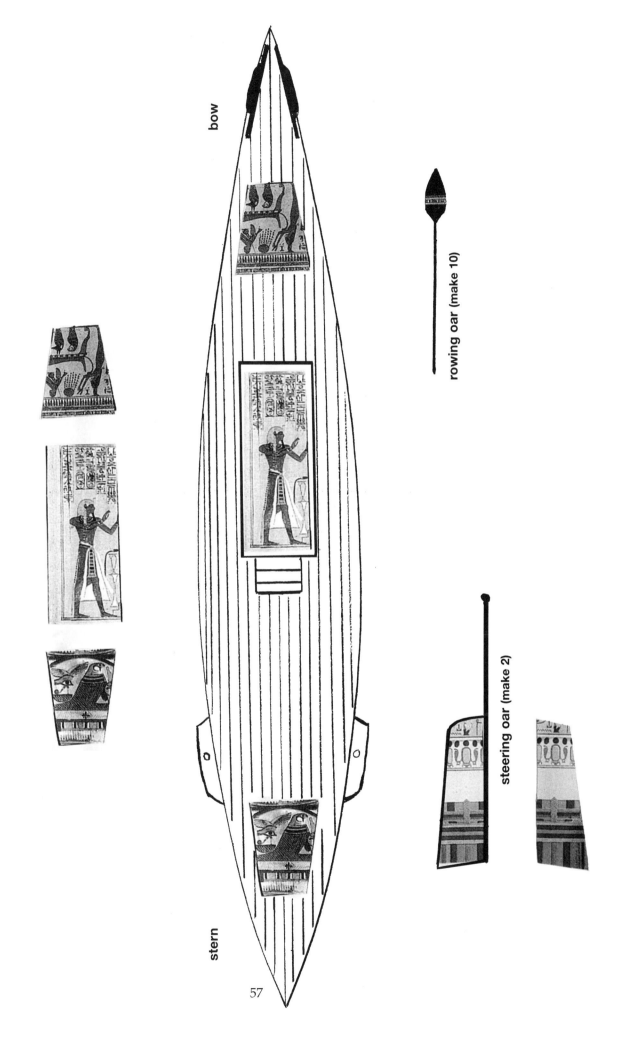

bow

stern

57

rowing oar (make 10)

steering oar (make 2)

SCALE DRAWING OF THE MODEL'S BASE STAND AND POTTERY SHARD

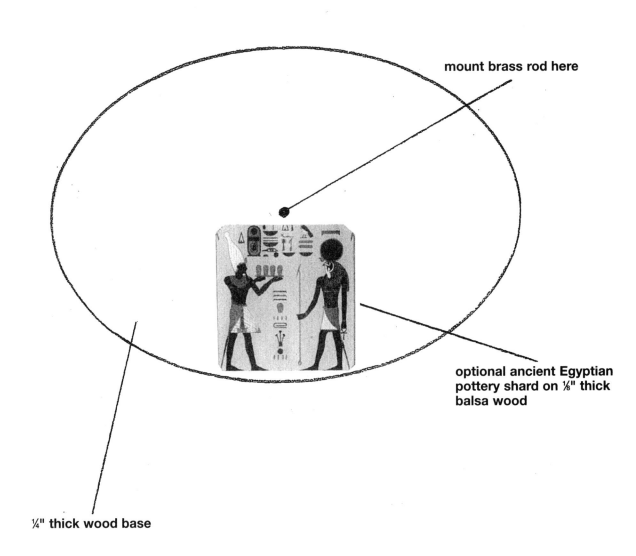

mount brass rod here

optional ancient Egyptian pottery shard on ⅛" thick balsa wood

¼" thick wood base

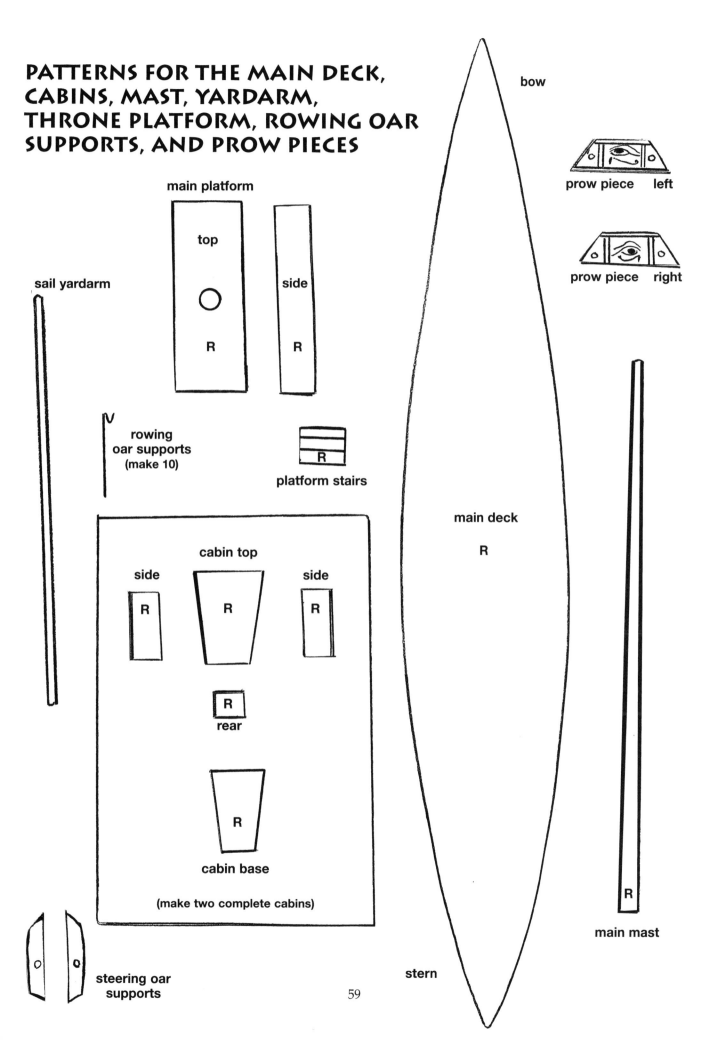

PATTERNS FOR THE MAIN DECK, CABINS, MAST, YARDARM, THRONE PLATFORM, ROWING OAR SUPPORTS, AND PROW PIECES

bow

prow piece   left

prow piece   right

main platform

top

R

side

R

sail yardarm

rowing oar supports (make 10)

platform stairs

R

main deck

R

cabin top

side

R

R

side

R

R

rear

cabin base

R

(make two complete cabins)

main mast

R

steering oar supports

stern

PATTERNS FOR THE HULL SECTIONS

3 left   R

2 left   R

1 left   R

main keel   R

1 right   R

2 right   R

3 right   R